For more than a generation Guenther has brought new foreign verse into our language. During the fifties and sixties editors recognized him as "the most active translator" of verse then appearing in little magazines.

In 1963, with Samuel Beckett and two other translators, Guenther collaborated on a volume of Alain Bosquet's *Selected Poems* published by New Directions/Lippincott. He also contributed to the Doubleday Anchor *Anthology of Spanish Poetry* (1961) and was represented by nineteen translations from seven French, Italian and Spanish poets in the Bantam anthology, *Modern European Poetry* (1966).

One of his papers, a first published study of the early St. Louis poet Pierre Francois Régnier, appeared in *The French in the Mississippi Valley* (University of Illinois Press, 1965). Other collections containing Guenther's work are *The Sea and the Honeycomb*, edited by Robert Bly (The Sixties Press, 1966) and *From the Hungarian Revolution* (Cornell University Press, 1966).

In 1967 the Rare Book Department of the Olin Library, Washington University, compiled a sixty-page bibliography of Charles Guenther's publications, excluding newspaper reviews and articles. For many years he reviewed, prolifically, books of verse and criticism for the *St. Louis Post-Dispatch*.

For three years Guenther taught creative writing at the People's Art Center in St. Louis, stressing the relations between art and poetry. Since 1955 he has led poetry workshops at various writers' conferences and he has served as assistant director (1966) and director (1970-71) of the McKendree Writers' Conference, Lebanon, Ill. He has also read and recorded his poetry, mostly in the West and Midwest.

Guenther is a former government translator, historian, geographer and supervisory cartographer. He lives in St. Louis where he is now employed as a supervisory librarian.

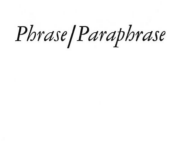

Phrase/Paraphrase

CHARLES GUENTHER

Phrase/Paraphrase

The Prairie Press : Iowa City

᚛

ACKNOWLEDGMENTS

The author thanks the Shell Companies Foundation for a
grant of assistance on this book, made through McKendree
College.

Twenty-five poems in this book, including three in the
Paraphrase section, have never been published before.

"Snow Country" and "Ste. Genevieve: Memorial Cemetery"
first appeared in the *St. Louis Post-Dispatch*. Special acknowledgment is made to David Ray and Cornell University Press
for permission to reprint "Cut and Run" from the anthology
From the Hungarian Revolution (1966).

Acknowledgment is also made to the following magazines
in which the other published poems have appeared: *Askance,
Audience, camels coming, Compass Review, The Cresset, Curled
Wire Chronicle, Edge* (Melbourne), *FOCUS/Midwest, Interna-
tional Anthology* (Athens), *Minnesota Review, The Nation, Par-
tisan Review, Poet Lore, Poetry* (Chicago), *Poetry Fund Journal,
Quartet, River, Sapien, Semina, South and West, Tambourine* and
The University Review.

For

HULDA C. GUENTHER

in loving memory

Contents

Phrase

Snow Country

In my mind there's a white country
with white trees
and black running brooks
and ponds stiff with reeds.
I take my sled again and go coasting
down the same hill where as boys
we went bellybusting, body piled
on body, breath on neck, eyes
stinging watery in the frosted air.

It was faster faster faster
we'd race and yell, urging the slope, coaxing momentum
like a runaway horse,
until—if we were lucky—the slowing sled careened
and we'd somersault shouting in heaps
through a snowbank, then arise
walking snowmen.

But now the hill is shorter and less steep
and the wind nips even through insulated clothes
and burns the ears and nose;
foot-flexed the sluggish runners ride
surfaces packed by cleated wheels
and not the least
riot enlivens this orderly winter.

What was the excitement of it? Each,
afterwards around the fire, with flaring cheeks
and warming the other. Nothing else.
Nothing? I remember now the steel tracks
and the lingering scream of a train in the icy night.
Down there was a second hill,
forbidden, where none of us ever coasted.
Now is the time to try it.

From *"Circle Search"*
For F. H.

A Job struck by infinite
pain will manifest
his grief and only fears it
won't faze us in the least.
When we see his plight,
the open sores, the bed of pains,
we'd better get used to the sight:
a man suffers and complains.

While he's hurt and still endures
incredible agonies,
plagues without cures,
we've seen patience exceed his:
he groused about his tortures.
You knew much worse than these.

Three Faces of Autumn

I

Now sunfire stains
the tupelos
and the shadows
in trapeziums
off the haybarns
straggle and gather
by rocks and birches
where the crickets'
still-fast whirr
cries against the closed
season

II

Harvest-heart
of autumn, vegetable
feast, harrowed
earth free
of horse and ox,
limbs released
of leaves except the still
green lilac and the red
rowanberry where
the waxwings pillage
and the pileated
woodpecker
taps the rotted
trunk

III

Irreducible
bones, boughs;
the wind dries after
the rain-drums; a flight,
geese over the first
hard glaze
and the hillside's
cry of the loon
while the chill
yellow light
dies

Six Picassos, One Ernst

The Acrobats (Picasso)

A fat man A frail boy
He heavy in wisdom He light in sin
Struck a rose and blue
Attitude on a box

Did this horned man
Procreate
That sky-haired nude
Innocence
Thin as it is
And will the red creature hold
For all plainly to see
The clear flesh in his grasp
And spoil it by his will?

Still Life with Skull and Leeks (Picasso)

With its own smell
Of decay long gone
This skull
Grins at the living
Pitcher The leeks
Lying unaired
By the locked window give
A new energy of death
To this cheekless

Dora Maar: Three Portraits (Picasso)

The cow the bull
The vegetable

Bare flesh strong
Nostrils and water-
melon breast

The last
Red and green striped
Torso and glad
Face depressed

Two Figures (Picasso)

Inscrutably
Weary and depressed
With secrets
Of love and poverty

They sit (unable
Perhaps even to buy
One drink one pipeful)
Blue and blue against blue

And stay
Far into morning
Until the café closes
And they must build their own fire

Clarinet Player (Picasso)

Green notes sounded
Downdraft in a
Slimy well
           Drawn
A deep song

But I'm in that well
Those mossy blocks
Aren't real Over me
There's a yellow mouth
Of a man who fingers
The keys
           And beckons
Consummate music

The Mirror (Picasso)

Her glass repeats
Face to face
Full
Profiled
Belly and breasts
Ovally
Doubled
The glass with her
Foretelling age

In gray
Blue purple
But the womb
Is green

Portrait (Max Ernst)

More flesh than eyes
Blue flesh
Volleys of motion
Her body ordered
As a bird stretched
In mist

And the print
Of bottle and bouquet

Buds of laughing and
Eyes quenched
In a wall of day

Tenson
(with commentary)

Poeta, volontieri
Parlerei a quei due che 'nsemo vanno.
—Inferno V
J'etais obscur au simple populaire;
Mais on dit aujourd'hui que je suis au contraire.
—Ronsard

Take a straight song Shun
circuit diluted wine
See the immodest sun
yield the strongest line—

Giraut who would forbear
poetry of the dark
dropped such a remark
adding upon the clear

—Sleep or be understood
Raimbaut you claim too hard
applause of the multitude
rime's only reward

But Raimbaut interposed
("virtuoso of form"
to whom legend supposed
Beatrix was warm)

—What if my song's not
thrown to the ends of the earth
is there any sot
can judge it what it's worth

No abundant dish
is ever delicate
Giraut—Damn me if you wish
I've salt on my plate

.   .   .

As Marcellus Giraut
overweeningly
indiscreet let go
praise of the Maccabees

though "a count's equal"
provoked a reprimand
from her he courted and
saw her buckler turn
                        The sequel

to Bernart the scullion for
he had loved Agnes
                        Caught
by the viscount he sought
tutelage of Eleanore

Guillem de Cabestanh
the countess Seremonde
loved ate his heart atoned
(relics at Perpignan)

And knave Guillem to whom
with mysterious pride
a trobairitz replied
All Provence knew the doom

of heretic chatelains
(but think of indigo-
eyed Lucinda's profane
commanded fandango)

Sing sing the prince of Blaye
sing Rousillon who ran
ruefully
       Dan dan
dan deridan deridan dei

Ste. Genevieve: Memorial Cemetery

The children find a game among the stones,
Searching for dates on them under the heavy trees;
Oak, pine and dark-fruited mulberries
Whose roots embrace and are nourished by the bones
Of the Vallés and the Roziers and the Linns.
A holiday. The town has sealed itself from the heat
Or gravitates to a park across the street,
Just within view, where a carnival begins

With a crash of popular music: visible lives
Divisible. Here by the spider and the mold
Children stop to eat mulberries. Blue and gold,
The day presents its trophies. The bee thrives.
The seasons' wheel gyrates and disappears
And memory withers from memorable acts,
Stripped to pairs of inconsequential facts
Sunk in a tended lawn for the pioneers.

You aren't mine, gentle people, except through the womb
Of Eve: infants, couples who took your vows
Together, but I love your coolness in the boughs.
Seasons are shadows whose continuum
Is to die. But how life flourishes there
For the silent, invisible, indivisible dead
In a corner of shade we think uninhabited,
Since no swan cries in this monumental air.

*E. E. C.**

E. E. would have given us
the roof of his treehouse
(the better to see the
      "   s   k   y   ")

let no one trespass there
to take from his Nature
for man-ready rifles
make man-loving neighbors

No painter of unmyths
he knew realistic
alias "anecdotal"
was NOT legal tender

nor was nonobjective
alias "abstract"
both MIScalled "art"
(two sides of the same coin)

the man of good humor
of tulips and chimneys
whose art was a question
of being alive

---

*"Thank you for asking if I want my name in lower
case: no, I do not."–Letter, January 17 '58

looked forward to back
a most meaningful birth
until a red tide
freed a miraculous flood

Elements

I think
all circles
gathering the world,
I gather earth
air fire water

and in the beginning

discover a fifth
element
arching over and
moving
the seasons

Birdcatcher

A flight bending
the reeds of
easy ponds seeks
asylum in the
cold horizon.

Under the noisy
flock a birdcatcher
trumpets but a
farther distance
calls them, an inner
wind torments them,
they weave unknowing
the tightest net
where feathers disappear,
from first to last
the sky lifts at
their isoceles
advance: a breathlessness
of birds.

Three Balloons/Flowers
On a portrait by Malinowski

Heat, light and air surround this girl or else
spring from her: red, yellow, blue. Balloons or flowers?
Only a hand implies a body; the face
is a flower, teeth-petaled, brow-styled.

Her eyes hold hurricanes
and suns simultaneously, calm
and chaos: might rock landslide-
like, or in smile burst, suddenly.

Twelve Pettisongs

Schooner (Feininger)

Flowing umber
topsail in precise
angles cleaving
blue and yellow

Loners (Paul Klee)

Only two
but not together
rather
walking alone into the dark
blue to the vivid sun

Birdcatcher (Paul Klee)

O the plumes
pink blue green
orange yellow brown
in a setting
of blood

Naked (Modigliani)

Oval
shoulders broad
hips
red purple black
fleshed lips

Girl (Modigliani)

Four-letter words:
look wish love girl

Mother/Child (Picasso)

Rosy brown mother
chestnut child
                    Was Jesus
white?

Pierrot (Picasso)

How the frail white-
costumed flesh in black
hat and pumps
quarrels with the dark
red green and brown
for dominion

Vase/Flowers (Picasso)

Can the flowers be more beautiful
than the vase
apparent in permanence
as a flashing swallow
blooms?

Bathers (Renoir)

Shimmering raw
fawn-fleshed
trio

Clown (Renoir)

My flesh
as clown:
pink and blue
joy among animals
clawing the sawdust

Boy (Rubens)

Pouting flushed
plump with dreams
still the encumbered
flesh of his mother

Sunflowers (Van Gogh)

Corps of yellow
green-yellow
brown
green
An attack of sunflowers

Attachments

The idea of man in space is fascinating:
over the atmosphere, thinner in relation
to the earth than an appleskin, he arched
from reality into mystery,
free in his motion, weightless.
                  In his vertical thrust
he lost all adhesion and
became immobile, until he contrived
cabins of artificial gravity.
He missed, you see, his attachments, a primitive
need at once obsessed him to hold fast
to something, for he didn't know
if he could cling to anything beyond.

Hero

Near this spot a hundred and ten
years ago a man named Whitey
Walker and his family
(wife, three boys, two girls)
died they say of thirst
or maybe exposure, huddled
together in the hot and cold
desert air.
                    And the wolves
picked them bare and even
the bones at last disappeared.

Now there's a new hamburger
house and the young jacks,
schoolboys down from Las Vegas,
pull aside in their Mustangs
every afternoon for milk
shakes cokes
and 68 flavors of ice cream
consumed in cool
air with stereo music;

or at a drive-in draw
up in pairs, squealing,
lifting the dust as their pony
cars peel out on the freeway,
playing chancier games where

the hero chicken loses
neck, guts and cock-
les—and the whole faculty
and student body mourn him and the high
school band plays at his funeral.

The Language Machine
Or, On First Looking Into Edmundson's *Proceedings of the National Symposium on Machine Translation*

After the scholars cull the homographs
Dismembering words by function (complex and plain)
Marking the beginning and end of paragraphs
Sentences quotes on sheets of cellophane
The format is established units fit
By text and context separate verbs that mean
One value syllables letters all of it
Goes into code and is fed in the machine
(Beast that needs and takes no breaks or lunches)
Which punches sorts prints punches sorts
Prints punches sorts prints prints
Prints punches punches sorts sorts
Sorts sorts prints prints prints
Punches punches punches

Helen at the Gate

"Well, now we'll be in better circumstances,"
The old Trojan muttered, watching Helen leave,
"But don't hold any malice, men, or grieve;
Just pardon her. See, she pays us with sweet glances.
For cities gain when they put aside their lances
And after the blood it's better to forgive—
I speak as a man, not as a conservative—
Thank God she's gone, the Greeks stop their advances."

Good councilor, they laugh at you, the younger
Hot-blooded boys moved to believe that there is
Some vestige of glory in the sword and scepter,
Their eager pulses quick with battle-hunger
That beat and bled for Helen and for Paris.
Oh Menelaus always should have kept her!

The Cuckold's Complaint
(traditional)

What were you doing at St. Paul's today?
—You wanted a son, so I went to pray.

But you stood in a corner out of sight.
—All churches are dark in the candlelight.

Well, I saw an army officer there.
—That was a figure of Christ, I swear.

Christ wears no ribbon for gallantry.
—That's His heart that was pierced on Calvary.

But Christ has *one* wound, in His *side,* you know.
—Some blood must have spilled up there from below.

And you don't talk to Jesus in that fashion.
—I was overcome with abiding passion.

I'll break your head like a china bowl.
—Then He'll have my immortal soul.

The Brown Rat

For Richard Eberhart

One March out on the asphalt road
A great brown rat lay in the sun.
Killed he was; my nostrils quivered,
Sensing the effects of his deliverance.
There humbly in the pungent air
He began a meaningless metamorphosis,
And horrendously my spirit shrank
At his organs spewed and turning rank.
Watching the birds pecking round him,
His body that stewed in its own fur,
Partly in disgust, partly in glee,
I gave the huge bloated thing a kick.
A cloud arose, grew into a fume
And Strength infused the atmosphere,
A vast olfactory disturbance,
And in my being a repugnant shudder.
The bloody corpse came not alive.
Then I remained in dumb aversion
Holding my breath as I did before;
And stanched the thirst for inquiry
Heaving in my unquiet soul
With a sickness in the abdomen;
Until I fainted on the spot
At the abhorrence of decay.
I recovered and left; and I came back
Bleary in the fall only to find

The fat brown creature flattened out.
But time had no significance,
And caught in rumination's trap
I had nor joy nor nausea,
Pent up in my sagacity.
Next spring took to the roads again
Bright and filthy, full of noise,
But halting where the brown rat was
Could find just a little bit of fuzz,
And the carcass sunk in an asphalt grave
Lovely as a mosaic;
I saw it as a photographer,
And mounted my long focus lens.
That was several years ago.
The great brown rat is gone now.
I stood in the clammy spring,
I clasped my empty stomach,
And thought of Pizarro, Cleon of Greece,
Of the Mogul's tomb where the Oxus flows,
Of Alexander and Lucrece
And Duke Alfonso left to the crows—
All poisoned shot stabbed choked or hung.

May their sainted corpses rot in dung.

Another Year

Hungary: a boy
stunted in his play
of climbing in the beeches,
whistling in the streets.

Hungary: a girl
never under freedom,
pleasing a new master,
old before her time.

Hungary: a man
strong with old desires,
sweating in the factory,
laboring in the fields.

Hungary: a woman
watching at her window,
waiting for a lover
who never comes.

Silences

The last words fall gently as a closing of blinds. All we can say of freedom merely restrains it. No instant or object, nor the events of your unleashing heart can be measured beside you. Absent you are present: our mouths share the wind.

When the living day disappears silence vacillates in the amber gardens. Flowers breathe colors. (We have already plucked the lilac of the tempest.) Sleep joyfully to the sound of the sun on your blue island of other silences. There is no festival but here.

Paraphrase

On Ssu-Ma Ch'ien's Shih-Chi

Once with his young wife
Ssu-ma Hsiang-ju bought a bar,
put on a pair of shorts
and slaved over the dishes
while she sat around and warmed her
                                    wine.

Two Songs from the Eskimo

Hunter

Why haven't I more skill?
Why can't I kill?
What stops me, what stops me?
Come my prey,
come my prey!
    O-o-o
    O-o-o-o!

Blue Sky

Oh summer heat warming the earth!
There's no breath of wind,
there's not a cloud.
Far off in the mountains
the reindeer grazes
on the blue skyline.
O joy,
O magic!
I sprawl on the ground and cry.

Measurements

We measure all with our meter
and we are beyond every dimension
of truth which is dream.
Shadow of a reflection morning flower
world's desire
in your room.
A window always
open to the view.
An all purple moon
that wheels around the universe.
Shadow of flowers
that burns doubly in the cold spring water.
The east.
Thought has pierced my heart.
My thought has taken wing
and travels.
Seas
bitter seas.
Drops and fragments of my pain
fluid automatic images.
What more do we wait for now
to hear Tiresias?

From the Modern Greek of Fivos Delfis

I Am the Same...

I am the same man
who healed the Levite
who took the whip
of his anger in his hands.
I am the same man
who was good, yet
threw his brother over the cliff
and built temples to love
and gallows.
I'm a beast: eternal
pain, life
good and evil
god and devil
Minotaur without egress
among the dark meanders
of the labyrinth:
and I still haven't known
my true self.
I am darkness and light
the brother of lions and wolves.

From the Modern Greek of Fivos Delfis

On the Hundred-Voiced Deserted Shore

Throw your stick in the sea
traveler.
The wind lifts your worn tunic
and your legs stagger.
Everything travels,
only you are motionless
as a stone.
Everything changes shape.
God's face
is an endless face
that you still don't know:
his soul is this wind
with a hundred voices
on the lonely crossroads
of pain,
it's this countenance
with a hundred masks.
Throw your stick in the sea.
What do you wait for, alone
on the deserted shore?

For some Ulysses to appear
who would bring you
the tempest of his dead heart?
The day turns light
The clouds roll,
the waves roll,

white flocks.
Metamorphoses of the moment
which hides and engulfs death.

From the Modern Greek of Fivos Delfis

Sestina for Lady Pietra

I've come to the dim light and the wide arc of shade
and at last to the whitening of the hills
where color disappears from the grass.
But my desire doesn't change its green;
it's rooted in the hard stone
that speaks and hears as if it were a girl.

Even so this young girl
stays frozen like snow in the shade
for she's not moved, except like a stone,
by the fair weather that warms the hills
and makes them turn from white to green
so it may cover them with flowers and grass.

When she crowns her head with a wreath of grass
she reminds me of no other girl
for she blends the curled yellow and green
so well that Love comes to stand there in the shade,
Love who sealed me in among low hills
more firmly than limestone.

She's more beautiful than a precious stone,
and the wound she gives no medicine made of grass
can heal; so I've run through plains and hills
trying to escape such a girl;
and in her light nothing can give me shade,
no hill, no wall, nothing green.

One time I saw her dressed in green,
so fashioned she'd have stirred a stone
with the love I have for her very shade;
then I summoned her in a field of grass,
as much in love as any girl
and hidden all around by the highest hills.

But rivers will surely flow up hills
before this wet green
wood catches fire, as a pretty girl
usually does for me; I'd pack off and sleep on a stone
all my life and go feeding on grass
only to see where her clothing gives shade.

No matter how darkly the hills throw their shade,
under her fine green a young girl
covers it as a man hides a stone under grass.

From the Italian of Dante

Midsummer Night

The black wind poured the night
into the little room.
Our bed was clouds broken
by silent lightning, a dark fragrance
of trodden grass, breezes
of wandering rain, a shower of leaves
from endless plains,
like an echo of sea waves.
Alone, in the confused
lightning in the troubled darkness,
your face was sickly pearl.

From the Italian of Diego Valeri

Inscribed On a Gravestone, Perhaps

Here far from everyone the sun beats down
on your caps and rekindles the honey in you,
and already the last cicada of summer
remembers us alive from its shrub,
and the siren that howls its profound
alarm over the Lombard plain.
O burnt voices of the wind, what do you want?
Tedium still rises from the earth.

From the Italian of Salvatore Quasimodo

Man of My Time

You are still that creature of the stone and sling,
man of my time. You were in the fuselage,
with the malicious wings, the sun-dials of death
—I've seen you—in the flame-throwing tank, on the gallows,
on the rack. I've seen you: you were,
with your exact science bent on extermination,
without love, without Christ. You have killed again
as always, as your fathers killed, as the animals
who saw you for the first time used to kill.
And this blood smells as in the day
when one brother said to the other:
"Let's go into the fields." And that cold, tenacious echo
has come subtly to you within your day.
Forgotten, O sons, the clouds of blood
risen from the earth, forgotten the fathers:
their graves sink in the ashes,
the blackbirds, the wind cover their heart.

From the Italian of Salvatore Quasimodo

Rose of Fire

You are the stuff of springtime, lovers,
the stuff of earth and water and wind and sun.
With mountains in your heaving breasts,
the blooming prairies in your eyes,

you spend your mutual spring
and even fearlessly drink the sweet milk
the slippery panther offers you
before he cruelly waylays you on the road.

Go, when the planet's axis
is inclined toward the summer solstice,
when the almond tree is green and the violet withers,

with thirst and the nearby source of springs,
to the concluded afternoon of love
with the rose of fire in your hand.

From the Spanish of Antonio Machado

Guitar

There will be a green silence
all made of guitars unloosened like hair

The guitar is a well
with wind instead of water

From the Spanish of Gerardo Diego

From "Asides from the Clowns"

How distant the soulmate
Who told me her good-byes
Simply because my eyes
Were degenerate!

Such a tender loaf,
At this moment she
Quite possibly
Spawns some little oaf.

For that fellow, no gallant,
They induced her to join
In wedlock has lots of coin,
But is poor in talent.

From the French of Jules Laforgue

The Schoolgirl

I know that roads advance
Faster than schoolchildren
Harnessed to their satchels
Rolling in the bird-lime of haze
Where autumn loses its breath
Never sweet to your studies
Was it you I saw smile
Daughter daughter I shudder

Weren't you wary
Of that unknown tramp
When he lifted his cap
To ask you his way
You didn't seem surprised
You approached each other
Like poppies and corn
Daughter daughter I shudder

He might drop
The flower he holds in his teeth
If he agrees to give his name
To return the wreck to the waves
Then some damned promise
Would haunt your sleep
In the shrubs of his blood
Daughter daughter I shudder

When that young man turned away
Night walled up your face
When that young man turned away
Bent back lowered brow and empty hands
You were serious under the willows
You never were before
Will he return your beauty
Daughter daughter I shudder

Do you know what was hidden
In the flower he had in his mouth
Father an unalloyed evil edged with flies
I veiled it with my pity
But his eyes held the promise
That I made to myself
I'm mad I'm born again
You're the one who's changing father.

From the French of René Char

Midnight Elegy

I jump out of my bed, a leopard on my back, a swift simoon
    silting up my throat.
—Oh if only I could collapse into blood and dung, into nothing!
I turn around among my books which watch me from the
    corner of their eyes
Six thousand lamps which burn 24 hours a day.
I'm standing, clear-headed, strangely clear-headed
And I'm handsome as a 100-meter runner. As a rutting stallion
    of Mauritania.
In my blood I carry a river of seeds to fertilize all the plains of
    Byzantium
And the hills, the austere hills.
I'm the Lover and the locomotive with the well-oiled piston.

Sweetness of her strawberry lips, thickness of her stone body,
    sweetness of her peach-secret
Her deep earth body open to the dark sower.
The spirit germinates under the groin, in the womb of desire
Sex is an aerial in the midst of the Multiple where flashing
    messages are exchanged.
The music of love, the poem's sacred rhythm can no longer
    pacify me.
Lord, I must summon all my strength against despair
—Sweetness of the dagger in the heart, up to the hilt
Like a remorse. I'm not sure of dying.

And what if that were hell, insomnia this desert of the poet.
This pain of living, this dying of not dying
The anguish of darkness, this passion for death and light
Like phalena moths at night on the hurricane lamps in the hor-
   rible rot of the virgin forests.

From the French of Léopold Sédar Senghor

Sometimes

Sometimes when a bird calls out
Or the wind barrels through the trees
Or a dog howls on a farm far away,
I stop and listen.

My soul turns back again:
A thousand forgotten years ago
The bird and the blowing wind
Were like me, they were my brothers.

My soul becomes a tree,
An animal and a cloud.
Transformed, it comes home as a stranger
And questions me. How can I answer?

From the German of Hermann Hesse

New Year's Eve

I lost my coat
But I don't freeze.
Watch me, friends,
And you'll conjure fire,
Rally with me
And you'll kindle flames.

I'm hot as a flue
Disgorging sparks,
A fire-spitting beast.
Like a roaring stove
I could fan my heat
Far out on the wind.

May I speak—
May I sprinkle away
These gleaming coals?
The New Year comes,
Heavy with lightning
And slumbering hope.

Fear wanders cold
In the wordless night;
I have no coat
But watch me glow!
Rally with me
To poke up fire,
To kindle hope.

From the Hungarian of Gabor Kocsis

Old Farmer

With heavy steps he walked across the hill
Where his hay died in lines, like verses;
His pipe—an imp with a fiery eye—
Lit up his copper-brown face.

He sat down. The silence grew around him,
Seaweed soaked in the blue lake of evening.
Maybe my mother's grandfather was like him,
A firebrand of embers who lasted ninety years.

Sometimes through his mustache a maimed word
Fell to the ground—little dark clods—
Tiborc's Lament . . .* perennial and timeless.

Meanwhile the lunar plow furrowed the air
In tiny particles through the new sown seeds
Sinking slowly, slowly toward the sky . . .

From the Hungarian of Gabor Kocsis

---

*Tiborc is the character of the oppressed peasant in Josef
Katona's play *Bano Bank* (1815).

Cut and Run

Endlessly a strange joy shakes in me, as
Endlessly the sea runs thundering to land, scattering
Foam over the rocks.
                    The waves' anger spends
Its final energy at my feet. Like a man revived,
I tremble in the wind, and stare around
At the steel-blue sea, the tepid bay, the green skies with white
        sails,
And beyond, the lazy ships. Gradually I realize
Here are no guards or guns or barbed-wire fences. I've come
To a clean, cool world. I've come from wastelands,
I've run from nightmares, from the dark into light, I've come
By magic seas to the stone-laced Norwegian coast;
And it's sweet to lie on rocks in the sun, to pierce
The soft waves, to swim in the deep, to drink
The summer, the clamoring sea, and the view; and I know
Freedom, my life's meaning.

From the Hungarian of Vince Sulyok

Colophon

This book has been designed and printed by
Carroll Coleman at The Prairie Press, Iowa City, Iowa. The
type is hand-set Garamond and the paper
is Warren's Olde Style.